CONTENTS

The Julian Stories
by Ann Cameron

CREDITS

Published by Scholastic Ltd,
Villiers House,
Clarendon Avenue,
Leamington Spa,
Warwickshire CV32 5PR
Text © Elaine Sturman and Jo Melhuish
© 1999 Scholastic Ltd
1 2 3 4 5 6 7 8 9 0   9 0 1 2 3 4 5 6 7 8

Authors Elaine Sturman and Jo Melhuish
Editor Steven Carruthers
Series designer Lynne Joesbury
Designer Rachel Warner
Illustrations Ann Strugnell
Cover illustration Ann Strugnell

Designed using Adobe Pagemaker

British Library Cataloguing-in-Publication Data
A catalogue record for this book is available
from the British Library.

ISBN 0-439-01648-7

The right of Elaine Sturman and Jo Melhuish to be
identified as the Authors of this work has been
asserted by them in accordance with the
Copyright, Designs and Patents Act 1988.

ACKNOWLEDGEMENTS

Penguin Books Ltd for the use of text and
illustrations from *The Julian Stories* by Ann
Cameron, illustrated by Ann Strugnell Text © 1981
Ann Cameron, Illustrations © 1981, 1999 Ann
Strugnell (1981, first published in the USA by
Pantheon Books as *The Stories Julian Tells*, first
published in GB 1982, Victor Gollancz/Hamish
Hamilton).

INTRODUCTION

The Julian Stories
by Ann Cameron

WHAT IS *THE JULIAN STORIES* BOOK ABOUT?

This book is a collection of six short stories. All of the stories are about Julian and his family and friends and all of them are told by Julian himself. The reader gets to know Julian's own views of the events and characters in each one.

WHAT'S SO GOOD ABOUT THE BOOK?

What is a catalogue cat? How can you grow a flower house? Can eating fig leaves make you taller? What have cave boys to do with loose teeth? How can you tell if somebody will make a good friend? These are some of the interesting questions you will be thinking about as you read Julian's stories about his life with his little brother Huey and his very special father.

ABOUT ANN CAMERON

Ann Cameron grew up in a small town of 7,000 people on a lake in Wisconsin, USA. She now lives in an equally small town of 7,000 people on the banks of another lake in Guatemala, Central America.

Ann has an exciting assortment of jobs. As well as being a full-time children's writer, Ann still manages to fit in caring for 24 very hungry cats, and performing her honorary role as supervisor of the Panajachel library, where she lives. In her garden, she has a lemon tree and loves to make fresh lemonade all year round from the fruit. She also like to sit and watch the hummingbirds buzz by and admire the wonderful view of the mountains she can see out of the studio window where she writes her stories.

Become a book detective

You can find out a lot about a book before you even read the first sentence. Here is the information our book detective found. Investigate front and back covers, title page, contents page and publication details to find out more. Write down answers to these questions and say what your evidence is for each answer.

How many stories?

Who is in the stories?

Who is the author?

This book is a collection of stories all written by the same author. Although the stories are separate, there are some things that they have in common. The pictures on the front and back covers tell us something about some of the stories. The book was first published in America in 1981 with a different title. This title gives us our first clue about how the stories are written. There are some more clues on the contents page.

What sort of things happen?

Which stories are illustrated?

Who is the storyteller?

What was the American title?

Prediction

*The Pudding
Like a
Night on the Sea*

'I'm going to make something special for your mother,' my father said.

This is the beginning of the book of Julian stories – the title of the first story and the first line.

● How do you think the story will develop? Write your ideas as answers to the questions. Look at the cover of the book if you would like some more clues.

Who is telling the story?

Who will be the main characters in the story?

Where is the story set?

What is the father going to make?

What might happen?

The Pudding Like a Night on the Sea

DIALOGUE AND NARRATIVE

● Read the story 'The Pudding Like a Night on the Sea'. Did you notice that it has lots of dialogue mixed with the narrative? Below is a passage of dialogue taken from the story. Read it through.

● What do you imagine happens while Julian and Huey are talking? Fill some of the gaps with narrative to describe how they look and what they do. The first one is done for you.

'Oh, it's a wonderful pudding,' Huey said.
He looked at me with his eyes shining and took a step closer. The pudding looked just like Dad said it would.

'With waves on the top like the ocean,' I said.

_____

'I wonder how it tastes,' Huey said.

_____

'Leave the pudding alone,' I said.

_____

'If I just put my finger in – there – I'll know how it tastes,' Huey said. *And he did it.*
'You did it!' I said. How does it taste?'

_____

'It tastes like a whole raft of lemons,' he said. 'It tastes like a night on the sea.'

_____

Descriptive language log

THE PUDDING LIKE A NIGHT ON THE SEA

This is the title of the very first Julian story. Straightaway, there is an interesting and unusual description which gets your imagination working.

● When you have finished reading each story, look through it and choose a few words or sentences which you think are interesting or different. Add them to the list below. You can continue your list on the back of this sheet.

Descriptive language	Title of story
It will taste like a whole raft of lemons.	The Pudding Like a Night on the Sea
We felt like two leaves in a storm.	

SEQUENCING THE STORY

● Read 'Catalogue Cats'. Here are some of the things that happen in the story, but they are muddled up. Cut them out and put them in the right order. Use the book to check your work.

Huey dreams about catalogue cats carrying a pumpkin.

Julian and Huey tell their father about the catalogue cats.

Huey writes a request for catalogue cats.

The catalogue arrives.

Julian's father says catalogue cats are invisible and they only do half the work.

Julian's father orders a catalogue.

Huey dreams the catalogue cats help in the house.

Julian tells Huey that catalogue cats jump out of the catalogue and help in the garden.

Julian says catalogue cats don't do that.

Julian feels scared.

Huey cries because there are no cats in the catalogue.

Our Garden

WHO WILL BUY.....?

● Read 'Our Garden' up to the part where Julian talks to the seeds. Julian and Huey have chosen two special things from the descriptions in the catalogue. What attracted them?

Genuine corn of the Ancients! This sweetcorn grows 20 feet high. Harvest it with a ladder. Surprise your friends and neighbours.

Julian liked the _____

because _____

_____

_____

Huey liked the _____

because _____

_____

_____

Make a house of flowers. Our beans grow ten feet tall. Grow them around string! Make a beautiful roof and walls out of their scarlet blossoms.

● Here are some questions gardeners might ask when they are deciding which vegetables to grow. Think of some more of your own and write them on the back of this sheet.

Does it need a lot of sun?   How long will it take to grow?
How often does it need water?
How much space will it need?   Will there be lots to eat?

Our Garden (2)

WHAT HAPPENS?

● Read the rest of 'Our Garden'. Have another look at the catalogue descriptions. Julian tells what happened to the sweetcorn and the house of flowers.

● Use one colour to highlight the parts that *actually happened* in the description below. Use another colour to highlight the things they *didn't expect* to happen.

And the sweetcorn did grow as high as the house, although there wasn't very much of it, and it was almost too tough to eat. The best thing of all was Huey's house made of flowers. After a while the flowers dropped their petals and turned into beans, and we ate the beans for supper. So what Huey made was probably the first house anyone ever played in and then ate.

● From your colours, decide if the descriptions were.... true?   partly true?   not true?

● How do you think Julian and Huey felt about their special plants?

Julian felt _____

because _____

_____

_____

Huey felt _____

because _____

_____

● Look again at the catalogue entries and at what happened.

Do you think the catalogue entries had enough information? Why were they written like this?

Because of Figs

Julian has some trouble because he believes what his father says. But the words people say are sometimes not exactly what they mean. Look at the diagram to see where the trouble starts. Some things happen to the fig tree and to Julian but Julian gets it all wrong! Fill in what Julian thinks is happening and what is really happening to the tree.

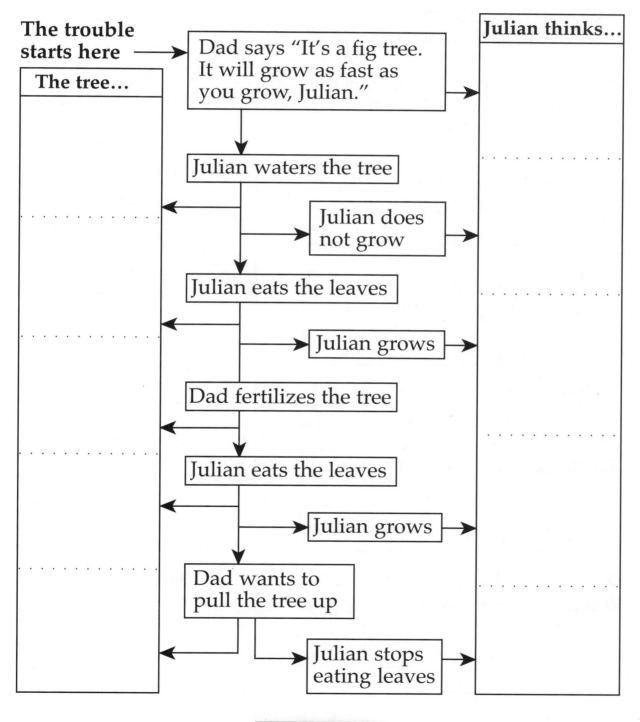

The trouble starts here →

The tree...

Dad says "It's a fig tree. It will grow as fast as you grow, Julian."

Julian waters the tree

Julian does not grow

Julian eats the leaves

Julian grows

Dad fertilizes the tree

Julian eats the leaves

Julian grows

Dad wants to pull the tree up

Julian stops eating leaves

Julian thinks...

My Very Strange Teeth

Julian doesn't want to wait for his tooth to fall out on its own. His family make some suggestions about what to do.

● As you read the story, fill in the chart about their suggestions.

● Think of some adjectives to describe how Julian feels about each suggestion. Write them in the last column.

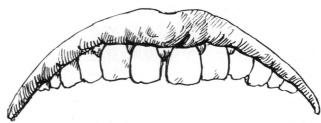

Who makes the suggestion?	What is the suggestion?	Will it hurt?	How does Julian feel?
Dad		yes	
Dad			
Dad			
Mum			
Huey			
Who makes the tooth come out?	**How does it happen?**	**Does it hurt?**	**How does Julian feel?**

● Do you notice a dramatic change in Julian's feelings? When and why does this happen?

Gloria Who Might Be My Best Friend

Gloria and Julian do become best friends. We can tell that they will by the things they say and by the things they do.

● Here are some things that help to make good friendships.

Describe how they happen in this story. Think of your friends and try to remember an example about them.

What makes a good friend?	In Julian's story	With my friends
Don't make fun of each other. page 63	Gloria doesn't laugh when Julian can't do a cartwheel.	
Show each other your special things. pages 65 & 66		
Laugh at the same things. page 66		
Speak politely to each other. page 65 – Julian		
Speak politely to each other. page 67 – Gloria		
Do things together. page 69		
	Julian does what Gloria says, although he doesn't know what she is planning.	
	Julian says he is sorry.	

Logging the stories

● As you finish each story, fill in this chart. Write the names of the characters and the places where each story is set. Answer the questions to fill in the other columns.

● When you have read all the stories, look at your completed chart. What patterns do you notice? What is the same about the stories? What differences are there?

● Talk to your partner about how the stories are the same and how they are different. Write some of your ideas on the back of this sheet.

Story	Characters	Setting	Is it mainly narrative or dialogue?
The Pudding Like a Night on the Sea			
Catalogue Cats			
Our Garden			
Because of Figs			
My Very Strange Teeth			
Gloria Who Might Be My Best Friend			

● You may like to use these words and phrases to help you.

Most of the stories ...	Only one story ...
We think it is interesting that ...	We are surprised that ...
but	although
whereas	usually
sometimes	...are the same because...
are different because ...	

Does Julian think he will get into trouble?	Does something unexpected happen?	Is there a misunderstanding?	Is it a funny story?

Misunderstandings

Words can cause a lot of trouble. They sometimes have two different meanings, or they don't mean what you expect them to mean.
Misunderstandings about words are an important part of some

of the Julian stories. Usually things get sorted out in the end.

In "The Pudding Like a Night on the Sea", Dad says:
"There is going to be some beating here now!
There is going to be some whipping!"

The brothers are upset because	They feel better when

In "Catalogue Cats", Julian says: "A catalogue is where cats come from... You open the catalogue and the cats jump out."

Huey is upset because	He feels better when

In "Because of Figs", Dad says:
"It's a fig tree. It will grow as fast as you grow, Julian."

Julian is upset because	He feels better when

Thinking about Julian's father

● Look at these adjectives and think about Julian's father. Use three different coloured highlighters to show how well each adjective describes Julian's father. You might think of some more adjectives to add.

Colour 1: he is always like that
Colour 2: he is sometimes like that
Colour 3: he is never like that

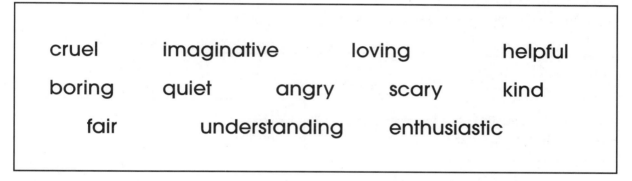

cruel	imaginative	loving	helpful
boring	quiet	angry	scary	kind
fair	understanding	enthusiastic

● Choose four of the adjectives highlighted in Colour 1 and find examples from the stories to fill in the chart.

Julian's father is...	Which story?	Quotation

● Write on the back of this sheet of paper. What would be good – and not so good – about having a father like Julian's?

Gloria Who Might Be My Best Friend

ANOTHER JULIAN STORY

● In this story, Julian makes five wishes. Some refer to stories we already know. Read them on Julian's list on page 68.

● You are going to write an extra Julian story about one of the other two wishes. Your "Logging the stories" chart gives you lots of information about things which are the same and different in the stories. Choose one of the story titles below. Use the chart to help you to plan your own story.

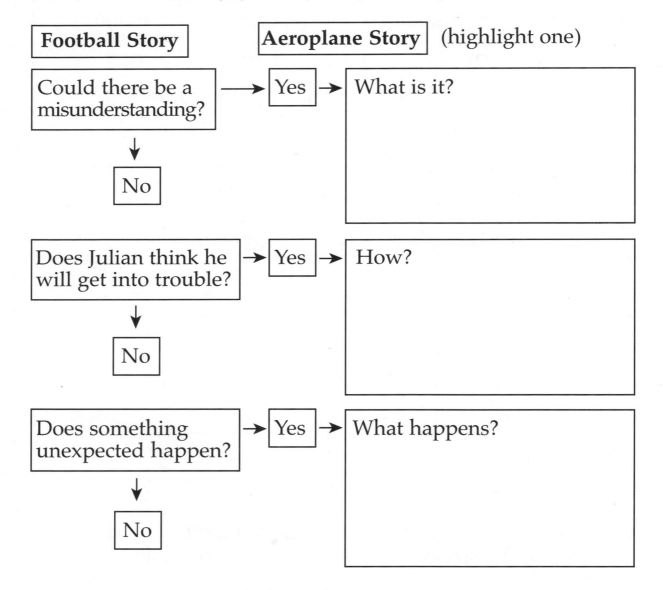

| Football Story | | Aeroplane Story | (highlight one) |

| Could there be a misunderstanding? | → Yes → | What is it? |
| No |

| Does Julian think he will get into trouble? | → Yes → | How? |
| No |

| Does something unexpected happen? | → Yes → | What happens? |
| No |

● Use this chart to plan your Julian story. Are there any funny bits?

1. Who is in the story?	2. What happens first?
Where are they?	

Julian could worry about getting into trouble here.

A misunderstanding could happen here.

Something unexpected could happen here.

3. What happens next?	4. How does it all get sorted out?

The Pudding Like a Night on the Sea

EATING PUDDING: A PLAY

● Find the work you did earlier adding narrative to Huey and Julian's dialogue. Work with a partner to change the scene into a play. The first part has been done for you. Continue to the end of the story using the back of the sheet, if necessary.

Scene: the kitchen

HUEY   Oh, it's a wonderful pudding!

JULIAN   With waves on top like the ocean.
               (Huey moves closer to the pudding.)

HUEY   I wonder how it tastes.
               (Julian pulls Huey's sleeve.)

JULIAN   *(in an anxious voice)*
               Leave the pudding alone.

_____

_____

_____

Making lemon pudding

● How did Julian's father make his special pudding? Would it be possible to make a real pudding from the information in the story? Write down everything you can find in the story about what you need (the ingredients) and what you do (the method).

A PUDDING

Ingredients

1. _____   3. _____

2. _____   4. _____

Method

1. _____

2. _____

3. _____

4. _____

5. _____

6. _____

7. _____

● If you were going to make the pudding, what else would you need to know to make sure that it turned out properly? Write out your questions and see if you can answer them by reading a recipe.

Catalogue Cats

HUEY'S STORY

Imagine Huey is telling the story of the Catalogue Cats. Think about having a big brother and how Huey would feel. Try to retell the story as if Huey were speaking.

Julian is my big brother. I think he is _____

If I don't know something, I ask Julian. He told me that a

catalogue _____

At first, I didn't believe Julian because _____

_____

I said I was going to ask Dad, but Julian _____

_____

At night, I dreamed that _____

_____

We had to wait ages for the catalogue. When it came, I felt

_____

There were no cats in the catalogue. I cried because _____

_____

Dad said _____

I felt better. I wrote _____

_____

VEG-U-LIKE

In "Our Garden" Julian, Huey and their father have different ideas about which vegetables to plant.

● Which vegetables do you think Julian's father would choose?

● Choose a vegetable and fill in the chart to show how important you think each statement would be to Julian's father.

	very important	important	not very important
He likes eating them.			
He likes cooking them.			
They will grow quickly.			
The neighbours will be impressed.			
They are easy to grow.			
They will look pretty.			
They will have lots of flavour.			
There will be plenty of them.			
They will grow enormous.			

● Write a catalogue entry that would attract Julian's father.

NARRATIVE

The story "Our Garden" is written almost entirely in narrative. Speech marks are used only once.

● Why do you think the author chose to write this story in this way? Here are some suggestions. Think about each one and decide whether you agree or disagree with it.

	Agree	Disagree	Not sure
It's good to have a change.			
It makes it easier to read.			
It makes it easier to write.			
It makes it more exciting.			
It makes you expect a different kind of story.			
It's better for reading out loud.			
It's better for reading to yourself.			
It has a different atmosphere.			

Gloria Who Might Be My Best Friend

A GOOD READ?

Publishers usually put a "blurb" on the back cover of a book to attract the reader. Look at the blurb for *The Julian Stories*. In just three sentences, you are going to write a blurb for the story "Gloria Who Might Be My Best Friend".

● Write one sentence about the main characters.

_____

● Write one sentence explaining a bit about what happens.

_____

● Write one sentence that will make readers want to know more. (Be careful not to give away the whole story.)

_____

Useful tip: you may be able to make your sentences longer and your blurb more interesting if you use some words like: when, so, who, because, that, if, although Sometimes a question or exclamation is good for the last sentence.

● Write your blurb out again, making sure your three sentences sound right together.

```
[blank box]
```

True or not?

● Do you think the Julian Stories are true or made up?
At the beginning of the book the author Ann Cameron writes:

> My thanks to Julian DeWette for sharing with me the childhood memories that inspired this book.

● Does this give you a clue? Have you changed your mind?

I think the stories are: true ☐   partly true ☐   made up ☐

● Why do you think that?

● Think about all the Julian stories you have read. Find and talk about: the best bit of dialogue; the funniest bit; the most interesting description.

My best bit of dialogue is...	I think the funniest bit is...	I like the description on page(s)...
page(s)...	page(s)...	because...
because...	because...	

USING THIS BOOK

MATCHING THE BOOK TO YOUR CLASS

The Julian Stories is a collection of individual stories, each with the same set of characters in similar settings. All the stories are told in the first person, so readers are given Julian's version of events and his perspective upon other characters. Such a collection of related but separate stories is a useful way of helping children to make the transition between picture books and chapter novels.

MANAGING THE READING OF *THE JULIAN STORIES*

The activities assume that the stories will be tackled in the same order as they appear in the book. Children could be encouraged to notice the cross-referencing between some stories.

Ways in (pages 4–5)

are prediction activities which should be attempted before reading any of the stories.

Making sense (pages 6–15)

has at least one activity for each story, to be attempted after reading, unless otherwise indicated in the Teachers' notes. The last activity (pages 14–15) is a logging chart covering all the stories, designed so that children can complete the relevant section after reading each story.

Developing ideas (pages 16–19) and Evaluation (page 26)

include further activities based upon individual stories and work designed to deepen understanding of the collection as a whole. These activities give children a purpose for rereading each story.

CLASSROOM MANAGEMENT

Most activities have been designed for flexible ways of working:
• individual – pages 7, 11, 16, 18–19, 22 and 26
• individual/pair – pages 4, 5, 8, 16 and 25
• small group – pages 6, 9–10, 12, 13, 20 and 24.

The group activities tend to address more complex or abstract ideas where a wider range of viewpoints would be helpful. Sharing and discussing ideas gives children the opportunity to develop their understanding.

The activities can be adapted to the structure of the Literacy Hour, such as:
• shared reading followed by independent work (individual/pair/group), eg, pages 6 and 9–10
• guided reading followed by independent work, eg, pages 4, 12 and 13
• shared writing followed by independent work, eg, pages 14, 16 and 18
• guided writing, eg, pages 25 and 26
• independent work, eg, pages 5, 8 and 11.

The 📖 icon indicates activities where children will need to refer closely to the text. These activities will be most successful if several copies of the book are available.

DIFFERENTIATION

The activities are designed to be used at the beginning of Key Stage 2. Although there is not a lot of text in the book, children who are not yet reading fluently may need additional opportunities to discuss and become familiar with each story before tackling the related activities.

Most of the children will be able to attempt the activities at their own level. The following pages, however, are likely to be particularly challenging for most children:
• page 13 – close reading and interpretation of the text
• page 17 – recognizing and understanding the idea of a common theme
• pages 18–19 – writing another story in the 'Julian' style

Some children may require support to complete these activities. Including a fluent reader within each group would help to make the activities accessible to all children.

Specific suggestions to help the children make the most of each activity are given in the Teachers' notes on pages 29–32.

TIME-SCALE

The book could be used as a focus for literacy work over two to three weeks.

This should allow time for all of the activities to be covered and for some to be worked on in depth. It is important not to exhaust the enthusiasm for the book by overworking the activities.

TEACHING POTENTIAL OF *THE JULIAN STORIES*

The activities fit the National Literacy Strategy *Framework for Teaching* for Year 3, covering text-level learning intentions in Term 1 and Term 3:

• to investigate how dialogue is presented
• to recognize key differences between prose and playscripts
• to write, read and present playscripts based on their own reading
• to be aware of different voices in stories
• to generate ideas using brainstorming
• to identify and collect specific descriptive words and phrases
• to express views about a story, selecting words/phrases to support their viewpoint
• to compare different stories; to evaluate stories and justify preferences
• to distinguish between first and third person accounts and write as first person account
• to consider the credibility of events
• to discuss characters' feelings, behaviour and relationships, referring to the text
• to compare and contrast works by the same author.

Additionally, the activities offer the following learning opportunities:

• to analyse the persuasive language of advertisements and to use it themselves
• to explore narrative order and the author's use of turning points in the plot
• to recognize the ways in which some written instruction (recipes) are typically organized and to write their own
• to write a story from another point of view
• to write a short, concise blurb.

SPECIAL TERMINOLOGY

It would be helpful if children had already been introduced to the following vocabulary:

• narrator
• narrative
• character
• text
• point of view
• image
• adjective
• short story
• dialogue
• ambiguity/pun
• quotation
• title page/contents page
• publication details/blurb.

RECOMMENDED CLASSROOM RESOURCES

You will need scissors and adhesive for page 8 and a variety of highlighter pens in different colours for pages 10, 17 and 18.

FURTHER READING

Books by Ann Cameron
Stories Huey Tells; Huey's Tiger; Julian, Secret Agent; Julian, Dream Doctor; Banana Spaghetti.

The Julian Stories

BECOME A BOOK DETECTIVE (PAGE 4)
Aim: to give some context to the reading and to support future reading choices.
Teaching points: Children will need to be familiar with the terminology (title page; publication details; blurb; contents). The activity provides an opportunity to talk about the book being a collection of stories about Julian and his family, as opposed to one continuous story or a book of separate short stories. Julian is the storyteller throughout and so the use of the first person is an important point. This may be new to children and need some discussion (author/narrator; point of view). 'Evidence' might be where the information is located or how it was deduced.
Extension: Children might categorize the books they are reading or have read (single story; one of a series; unrelated stories; closely related stories; novel with chapters, and so on).

PREDICTION (PAGE 5)
Aim: to establish the environment of all the stories and to predict the content of the first one.
Teaching points: Children could consider the knowledge they are drawing on to make predictions (both directly from the text and illustrations and indirectly from previous knowledge of story forms). They might also think about the elements which are likely to be common to all stories, such as storyteller, characters, setting.

MAKING SENSE
THE PUDDING LIKE A NIGHT ON THE SEA: DIALOGUE AND NARRATIVE (PAGE 6)
Aim: to investigate dialogue and narrative.
Teaching points: If the children have not worked on dialogue and narrative before, this activity could be preceded by
• adding speech bubbles to pictures (such as the full page illustration at the beginning of the story)
• photocopying an appropriate passage and highlighting narrative and dialogue in different colours.
   Children should have plenty of opportunities to discuss what narrative does (describes what

characters do and how they feel) and how it is written (in the past tense) before they attempt their own writing.
Extension: Children could read out their work with different people taking the parts of each character and the narrator. How will Julian (who is both narrator and participator) be played?

DESCRIPTIVE LANGUAGE LOG (PAGE 7)
Aim: to support language development by encouraging personal collections of words and phrases.
Teaching points: General discussion of what makes words and phrases particularly effective would be helpful before children embark on their own choices.
Extension: The two examples given are similes – if appropriate, specific work on similes could slot in here.

CATALOGUE CATS: SEQUENCING THE STORY (PAGE 8)
Aim: to encourage close reading and understanding of the story by sequencing main events.
Teaching points: The sentences are deliberately written with similar vocabulary and without connectives so that children will have to read each one carefully. They will need to refer to the story for support.
   An additional task could be to add connectives where appropriate to make the text flow.
Extension: Children could be asked to think beyond the text and explore Julian's own understandings. Does Julian think catalogue cats exist? Does he change his mind? They may need to be supported with some suggestions, such as
• he doesn't know what a catalogue is
• catalogue starts with cat
• he doesn't want Huey to think he doesn't know something
• he thinks there are cats in catalogues.
   Children should consider particularly the effect on Julian of Dad's intervention. It may be difficult to separate what Julian might think (perhaps

catalogue cats do exist if Dad says so) from a reader's reaction (Dad doesn't want Julian to lose face or Huey to feel let down).

OUR GARDEN: WHO WILL BUY? (PAGE 9) AND WHAT HAPPENS? (PAGE10)

Aim: to examine persuasive language.

Teaching points: The two sheets are designed to be copied on to A3 so that the 'before' and 'after' text extracts can be examined together. The writer's choice of words and anticipated reader reaction needs discussion. 'Genuine corn of the Ancients!' refers to the introduction of corn to European settlers by Native Americans. Children might consider this interesting point in the light of their 'detective' work (the book was first published in America). The activity sheets raise the issue of deliberate omissions in adverts, which could be explored in other contexts. Children may need help in brainstorming ideas about what one needs to grow good vegetables.

The aspect of the intended audience and why Julian's father is not interested in the sweet corn or beans is addressed further in Our Garden: Veg-U-Like (page 23).

Extension: Children might think about illustrations to accompany the catalogue entries that would add to their attractiveness and/or look at actual adverts in terms of choice of words, omissions in information and intended audience.

BECAUSE OF FIGS (PAGE 11)

Aim: to look closely at Julian's misunderstandings and analyse their effect on the story.

Teaching points: This story hinges on Julian taking literally his father's words about growing. The activity focuses on how Julian's mistaken thinking grows and how it influences his actions. The second part of the activity looks at the reality of the situation. Give children other examples of how taking things literally leads to misunderstanding. Is this particularly characteristic of young children? There is a similarity to 'Catalogue Cats' when Huey takes what Julian says literally.

MY VERY STRANGE TEETH (PAGE 12)

Aim: to look for specific details in the text and to infer feelings.

Teaching points: Children will need to understand what a suggestion is and that it usually evokes a response. The mother's suggestion (that having two teeth is special and would have been an asset to a prehistoric caveman) brings about a dramatic turn in the story and how Julian feels. For the final column, it might be useful to brainstorm possible adjectives to encourage children to extend their vocabulary (for example 'worried', 'apprehensive', 'disappointed').

Extension: This is a good example of a story which hinges on a pivotal point. The whole emphasis changes when Mum suggests that keeping the tooth might be a good idea. Children could list examples from their wider reading of other stories which have a similar pattern.

GLORIA WHO MIGHT BE MY BEST FRIEND (PAGE 13)

Aim: to locate and paraphrase particular references in the text and to draw on own experience

Teaching points: The opening paragraph of the story raises issues of stereotyping. Children might work in same-sex pairs and list activities that girls like/boys like/both like. The pairs could come together (two boys and two girls) to discuss and modify their ideas. A plenary would be needed to draw out the issues and challenge any stereotypes. The activity sheet first asks children to search the text closely for specific examples of friendly behaviour. The last two examples ask them to think of a phrase to describe the behaviour (for example 'Trust each other' and 'Be able to apologize'). You may need to guide less experienced children where to look. Before or after completing the final column, children could brainstorm their own ideas about what makes a good friend.

Extension: Children might write about their memories of making a friend.

LOGGING THE STORIES (PAGES 14–15)

Aim: to pinpoint factual and stylistic features in all the stories.

Teaching points: The two pages should be photocopied together onto A3 paper. The column headings cover straightforward and more complex

features so that children can start to consider similarities and differences in all the stories. You may find it useful to tackle Misunderstandings (page 16) before this chart. We have suggested a linear completion at the end of reading each story, but it would also be valuable to use this chart to reflect on all the stories and fill it in vertically. Children could highlight the main character(s) and setting where they have listed more than one. Some words in the question headings (trouble? unexpected? misunderstanding?) draw attention to some common features – you may want to identify others. Children need to be aware that answers in these columns will be 'no' for some stories and 'yes' in more than one case for others.

It is important that children interpret the information they have gathered, for example the restricted nature of character and setting. It would be good to explore orally the language of comparison and to model complex sentence structures before grappling with the writing activity. The words and phrases given are not exhaustive and could be added to in discussion.

The order of the stories would also be an interesting discussion. How important is the order? What effect would changing the order have?

Extension: This activity could be used as the basis for more formal work on story structure (including terms such as 'straightforward recount'; 'pivotal point'; 'flashback').

DEVELOPING IDEAS
MISUNDERSTANDINGS (PAGE 16)

Aim: to explore common themes in the stories.
Teaching points: This activity depends on children having a thorough knowledge of the stories and being helped to recognize that misunderstandings are a common thread in several stories. Misunderstandings are commonly associated with young children (compare *Cider with Rosie* by Laurie Lee) and they may well have examples from their own family experiences.
Extension: A known example could be written, with or without prior discussion.

THINKING ABOUT JULIAN'S FATHER (PAGE 17)

Aim: to work on a character profile with reference to the text.
Teaching points: You may like to brainstorm suitable adjectives, and discuss how the character is developed through the stories, before giving out the worksheet. Children should be encouraged to find actual quotations from the stories to support their observations.
Extension: Children could use their sheet to write a paragraph profiling Julian's father.

GLORIA WHO MIGHT BE MY BEST FRIEND: ANOTHER JULIAN STORY (PAGES 18–19)

Aim: to write a story in the style of *The Julian Stories*.
Teaching points: Children could begin by thinking about both a football and an aeroplane story (perhaps using two copies of page 18) and then choose the one they prefer to continue with the structured planning on page 19. Remind the children that the questions they are considering in planning their story refer back to the Logging the Stories chart (from pages 14–15). Encourage them to include detailed ideas for at least one of the elements on page 18. Page 19 then provides a more formal planning structure into which these ideas can be incorporated at one of the indicated points (but not all of them).

THE PUDDING LIKE A NIGHT ON THE SEA: EATING THE PUDDING: A PLAY (PAGE 20)

Aim: to explore the conventions of playscripts.
Teaching points: Preliminary work for this activity is in The Pudding Like a Night on the Sea: Dialogue and narrative (page 6).

Ideally, give children an extract from a playscript and ask them to identify the conventions (page layout with character names down the left side of the page; dialogue to the right with no speech marks; starting a new line for each character; directions in brackets and written in the present tense, and so on). Discuss how dialogue, stage directions and characters' actions/

feelings are presented and how this relates to the dialogue/narrative distinction. IT could be used to enhance layout (italics are conventionally used for stage directions).

Extension: If the children prepare their play for performance, there is an opportunity to consider the role of the director.

MAKING LEMON PUDDING (PAGE 21)

Aim: to practise instructional language.

Teaching points: Children will need to read recipes and become familiar with the conventions of the language and layout used. They can think about the difference between describing the pudding in the story and in a recipe (what is and isn't important). Comparison with a printed recipe for lemon pudding/mousse would help to make the points clear.

Extension: Differences in spoken and written instructions could be explored (How would you explain the recipe to a friend? How are you changing the language?).

CATALOGUE CATS: HUEY'S STORY (PAGE 22)

Aim: to rewrite a story from another point of view.

Teaching points: It may be useful to precede this activity with a discussion of sibling relationships in general and Huey and Julian in particular. *The Stories Huey Tells* (also by Ann Cameron) could be read to give more idea of Huey's character.

The writing frame supports the writing for children who may need it. Encourage them to see the frame as a whole and to organize their writing appropriately. The layout is a guide only – the amount of writing in each section will vary.

Extension: Children could also write the same story from Dad's perspective or, for example, 'The Pudding Like a Night on the Sea' from Mum's point of view.

OUR GARDEN: VEG-U-LIKE (PAGE 23)

Aim: to write a catalogue entry using persuasive language for a particular audience

Teaching points: Preliminary work is in Our Garden: Who will buy? and What happens? The box-ticking activity will help the children focus on what they think Julian's father would look for when choosing seeds. Make sure the children use

this information in their catalogue entry. They will also need to think about form - the sweetcorn and bean entries will be a useful guide (number and length of sentences, enthusiastic tone, exclamations and questions, capital letters for emphasis). IT can be used – font, size of print, layout of words and pictures.

OUR GARDEN: NARRATIVE (PAGE 24)

Aim: to consider the effect of narrative writing.

Teaching points: Some children may feel able to tackle this activity on their own or in a pair. Others may benefit from a wider group discussion linked with hearing this story and a contrasting one ('The Pudding Like a Night on the Sea' or 'Catalogue Cats') read aloud.

Extension: Children could find other stories that are predominately written in narrative or dialogue and discuss their preferences for listening to and for writing themselves.

GLORIA WHO MIGHT BE MY BEST FRIEND: A GOOD READ? (PAGE 25)

Aim: to support short concise writing in a particular form.

Teaching points: Children need to understand that a blurb:
* makes you want to choose the book
* is interesting in its own right
* is short (so every word has to count)
* doesn't give away the plot
* leaves you wanting to know more (by using exclamations, questions or ellipses).

Children need to read and consider blurbs from familiar and unfamiliar books.

EVALUATION
TRUE OR NOT? (PAGE 26)

Aim: to consider the nature of fiction.

Teaching points: Children may or may not have noticed the dedication. How important is it to know that there was a real Julian? Does it change one's attitude to the stories?

Extension: Children could consider how to make a recount of a fairly mundane experience interesting and exciting for the reader as *The Julian Stories* do. Remind them of key words such as dialogue, description, humour and feelings.